IRELAND

ENCHANTED ISLE

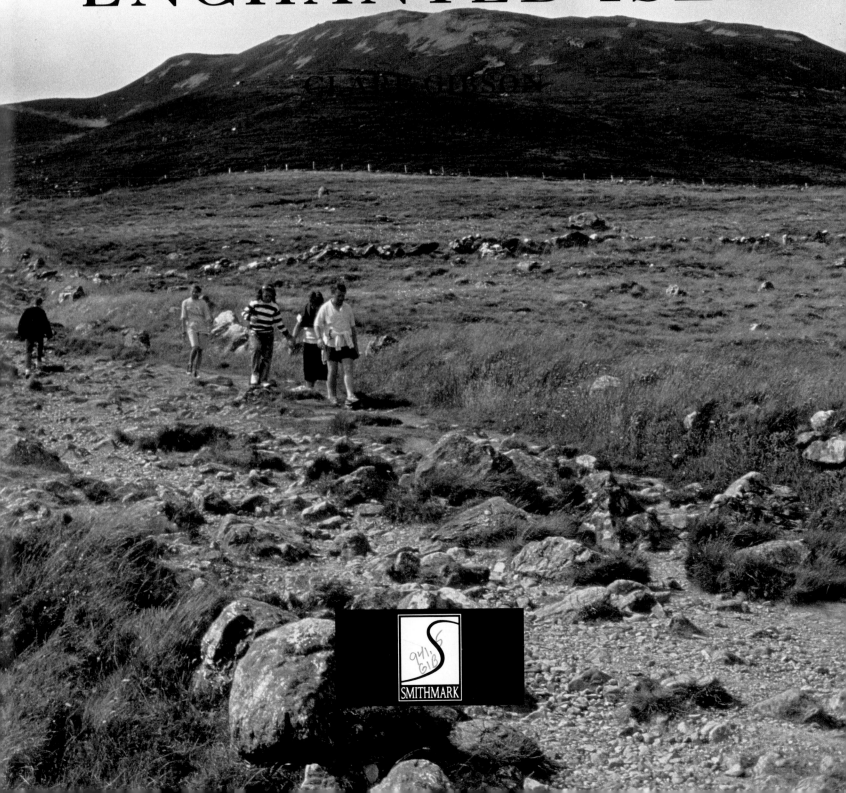

IRELAND
ENCHANTED ISLE

CLARE GIBSON

SMITHMARK

PG DM JC MB BD CCC

This edition published in 1995
by SMITHMARK Publishers Inc.,
16 East 32nd Street,
New York, New York 10016

SMITHMARK books are available for bulk purchase
for sales promotion and premium use. For details
write or telephone the Manager of Special Sales,
SMITHMARK Publishers Inc., 16 East 32nd Street,
New York, NY 10016. (212) 532-6600.

Produced by Brompton Books Corp.,
15 Sherwood Place,
Greenwich, CT 06830

ISBN 0-8317-3492-2

Printed in China

10 9 8 7 6 5 4 3 2 1

Page 1: The coastline of Bundoran, one of County Donegal's oldest and most popular seaside resorts, where fantastically shaped cliffs and rocks protect the superb sandy beaches.

Pages 2-3: Legend has it that St. Patrick prayed and fasted for the 40 days of Lent on Croagh Patrick in County Mayo. Today Ireland's "holy mountain" is popular with hikers, as well as pilgrims.

Below: A ruined cliff-top fortress in County Clare is dramatically silhouetted against a lowering sky.

Opposite page, below: Lying off the Iveragh Peninsula in County Kerry are the sharp rocks known as the Skelligs. Their name derived from the Gaelic word *sceilig*, meaning "splinter of stone," the Skelligs comprise Small Skellig (a haven for gannets), and Great Skellig or Skellig Michael. Skellig Michael, whose pinnacle rises 700 feet above sea level, housed an inaccessible monastery from the sixth to the twelfth centuries.

Page 7: By building up its poor soil, the people of the Aran Islands, 30 miles off the coast of Galway, have enabled the otherwise barren land to support cattle. These are penned in by means of the many low, handbuilt stone walls that traverse the island.

9.98

CONTENTS

INTRODUCTION

IRELAND IS A LAND OF fascinating paradoxes: its landscape juxtaposes bleakness and lusciousness, while its history is one of turbulence and tragedy, of repression and rebellion, yet also of hope and fortitude. Clearly, in order to appreciate the country and its people fully, one must to try to understand its rich and troubled history.

Although Ireland's origins are shrouded in the mists of time, it has been inhabited for at least 8000 years. However, of all the early settlers, it was the Beaker people – the *Tuatua Dé Danaan* – who left the greatest mark. Dedicated to the goddess Dana, legend has it that after their defeat by the invading Celts in around 500 B.C. their mystical arts enabled them to survive to this day as "fairy people." Ireland was never invaded by the Romans; instead the Celts (or Gaels) were the first successful invaders from Europe, eventually forming Ireland's indigenous population. Their success was largely due to a highly organized social structure, in which their various clans were each ruled over by a petty king, who in turn owed allegiance to the High King (*Ardrí*) in the centralized kingdom of Tara (established by King Niall of the Nine Hostages, who ruled in the late fourth century). Within the clans themselves an astonishingly detailed class system prevailed, consisting of free men, professionals, and slaves. By the early Christian era, the Celts had consolidated their power, and had established the Five Kingdoms of Ireland – Ulster, Meath, Leinster, Munster and Connaught – which closely correspond to today's provincial divisions of Leinster, Munster, Connaught and Ulster.

In 432 St. Patrick arrived in Ireland, bringing with him the flame of Christianity which, once kindled, would wield such overwhelming influence over Irish history and culture. The sympathetic assimilation of pagan practices helped assure the success of the new religion. The monastic system became particularly strong, and was accompanied by the fervent missionary zeal which sent St. Columba to Iona. Irish monks were renowned for their learning and artistry and, when the rest of Europe was under the thrall of the barbarian Dark Ages, were responsible for keeping Christianity alive.

However, for centuries the monasteries themselves were constantly under threat from another invading force: the marauding Vikings. By means of the skillful navigation of Ireland's waterways in their longboats, the Vikings were able to penetrate Ireland's heartland and carry off precious artifacts from the vulnerable monasteries. Although they later established trading colonies (such as Dublin and Cork), the Vikings were finally defeated by the *Ardrí* Brian Boru in 1014 at the battle of Clontarf.

Despite this success, infighting between the clans later crystallized into serious disunity, making Ireland ripe for exploitation. In 1152 Devorgilla, the wife of Tiernan O'Rourke of Breffni, was abducted by Dermot MacMarrough, King of Leinster, thus starting a quarrel which resulted in Dermot's alliance with the powerful Anglo-Norman Earl of Pembroke ("Strongbow") – an alliance which then led to the victory of the elite Norman forces at Waterford in 1169. In accordance with feudal custom, in 1172 Strongbow's overlord, King Henry II of England, asserted his sovereignty by force. For the next 800 years Ireland would be a battleground fought over by the forces of domination and independence.

Despite the nominal subjugation of the Irish by the Anglo-Normans, in practice the Gaelic lords in the north and west remained relatively independent, leaving only the territory around Dublin – "the Pale" – under the control of the conquerors. Although Henry VIII proclaimed himself "King of Ireland" and tried to introduce his reformation into the country, it would be the reign of Elizabeth I which would mark a turning point in the relatively laissez-faire Irish policy of the English monarchs up to then.

Elizabeth I was determined to master Ireland, sending her favorite, the Earl of Essex, to suppress a major revolt led by Hugh O'Neill and Red Hugh O'Donnell of Ulster. Essex's failure doomed him to death, but in 1600 Lord Mountjoy arrived in Ireland, brutally smashing risings in Munster, and defeating a Spanish armada which had come to O'Neill's aid at Kinsale in 1601. Shortly afterward, in 1607 (in the reign of James I), the rebel Irish lords were forced to flee abroad. Facing no organized resistance, James I consolidated his victory by implementing strict anti-Catholic measures, including a system of plantations which apportioned Catholic-owned land to Protestant Scottish and English settlers.

The outbreak of civil war in England, and the alarming prospect of Puritan rule, motivated the Irish to support Charles I and, after his execution, Charles II, and rebel in support of the Royalists. Cromwell's vengeance was ruthless, and by 1650 he had left Ireland broken and beaten. Yet in 1688 Ireland rose again, in support of the Catholic James II. For a while Ireland became the backdrop for the "Glorious

Revolution," culminating in the battle of the Boyne in 1690, in which James and William of Orange – personifying the forces of Catholicism and Protestantism – fought for England's throne. James's defeat spelled further punishment for the Irish, and the next century would see the Catholic population crushed by the draconian Penal Laws, which forbade them to own land.

Although beaten, the Irish were not cowed. Encouraged by the success of the American and French revolutions, and with armed French support, Theobald Wolfe Tone led a rebellion of "United Irishmen" against the English. However, the rebellion's failure was rendered absolute in 1801, when the Act of Union establishing the United Kingdom of Great Britain and Ireland abolished the Irish parliament, instead allocating Irish representatives seats in the British House of Commons in London (from which Catholics were barred). Irish Catholics would remain unrepresented until 1829, when the election of a Catholic, Daniel O'Connell (the "Liberator") forced through the Catholic Emancipation Act.

In 1846-47, Ireland was struck by the Great Famine: a potato blight which had disastrous consequences for the ordinary Irish peasant, whose staple diet consisted of six pounds of potatoes and a pint of milk a day. One million people died, and a further million emigrated on squalid "coffin ships" to England and America. The hold of the motherland remained strong, and emigrants would keep alive the spirit of hatred against British rule.

By the end of the nineteenth century, British politicians were becoming more amenable to the concept of Irish home rule, influenced by men such as Charles Stewart Parnell, leader of the "land war" which had brought down the tyrannical landlord structure. However, Gladstone's home rule bills of 1886 and 1893 were rejected, while the passage of that of Asquith in 1914 was disrupted by the outbreak of World War I. In 1916 Irish frustration found its tragic expression in Dublin's Easter Rising.

With the end of World War I in 1918, however, came the end of Irish submission. In 1918 elected Irish representatives affirmed Ireland's independence – heralding three years of fierce guerrilla fighting between the forces of the Crown and *Sinn Féin* (led by the American-born Eamon de Valera). Finally, in 1921 the Protestant-dominated, northern Unionists, who had no wish to break away from Britain, established a parliament for the six northeastern counties. In the south, the remaining 26 counties – now known as the Irish Free State – were granted dominion status and their own house of representatives (the *Dáil Éireann*). Home rule had at last been achieved.

Since the 1920s, the two Irelands have followed separate paths. A new constitution in 1937 gave southern Ireland a republican government and a new name – *Éire* – and in 1949 it finally severed all its links with the British Commonwealth. Northern Ireland remained within the United Kingdom. The passing of the 1949 Northern Ireland Act prompted rising Irish Republican Army (I.R.A.) agitation, reaching crisis point with the civil disturbances of 1968, after which British troops were brought in. In 1972, at the height of "The Troubles," the parliament of Northern Ireland was suspended, and since then Ulster has been governed directly from Westminster through the British Secretary of State for Northern Ireland. Despite initiatives such as the 1985 Anglo-Irish Agreement to try to reach a settlement, the following years saw extremist terrorists such as the I.R.A. and the Ulster Defence Association (U.D.A.) continue to wage war upon each other, and upon those unfortunate innocents caught in the crossfire. However, the consequences of the 1993 Downing Street Declaration have brought the first real glimmer of hope for a lasting peace in 25 years. Despite the terrible legacy of its past, Ireland has emerged strong and positive. Emigration figures have fallen, and its highly educated youth are determined to achieve a peaceful and prosperous future for themselves and their children.

LANDSCAPE

THE WESTERNMOST ISLAND of the European continental shelf, if one follows a diagonal line from Fair Head in the northeast to Crow Head in the southwest, Ireland is only 480 km long and 189 km at its widest. However, this compact Atlantic island contains an amazing diversity of geographical features, flora and fauna – a result of Ireland's gentle climate and unique physical make-up.

At the heart of Ireland lies a vast limestone plain which comprises huge areas of bogland (such as the Bog of Allen in County Offaly), low hills (drumlins), and hundreds of Ireland's 800 lakes and rivers, including the mighty 200-mile-long Shannon. Surrounding this central plain are impressive hills and mountains: red sandstone rocks in the south and southwest; limestone and shale along the western coast; in the west itself mountains of volcanic, quartzite and granite rock; while the northeast consists of a massive basaltic plateau. Ringing these highlands in turn is a ragged, 3000-mile-long coastline, unparalleled in its drama, along which craggy rock cliffs give way to lonely sandy bays. The ice age left its mark on Ireland, as can be seen in glacial valleys such as the Connor Pass in County Kerry, while the extraordinary "stepping stones" of the Giant's Causeway in County Antrim were formed by the cooling and contraction of molten lava 60 million years ago.

Each of Ireland's four provinces can claim areas of unique, but differing beauty. Leinster is characterized by its soft, fertile land, its peat-rich bogs, moors and grassland, and the imposing granite splendor of the Wicklow Mountains. Munster is

perhaps the most scenic of the provinces, containing as it does the Burren, (a limestone desert which harbors Mediterranean, Arctic, and Alpine plant species), and the Macgillicuddy's Reeks, including Carrauntoohil, Ireland's highest peak. Within the famous Ring of Kerry are the lakes of Killarney and the Dingle coastline, and to the north the forbidding Cliffs of Moher. Nestling between this rocky grandeur can be found exquisite beaches, such as Bantry Bay's, with its seals and tropical plant life. In contrast, Connaught is a remote and infertile province, yet its very desolation inspired Ireland's greatest poet, W. B. Yeats. The Twelve Bens of Connemara and the Maumturk Mountains of County Galway are rivaled by the Knocknarea and Benbulbin Mountains in County Sligo, while Croagh Patrick – Ireland's "holy mountain" – radiates symbolism. Ulster is dominated by Lough Neagh, the largest lake in the British Isles, yet can also boast the lakes of Fermanagh, mountains such as Slieve League, and breathtaking glens, such as those of Antrim.

The Gulf Stream ensures that the weather is mild (even in winter), and this moderate climate has its startling result in the growth of subtropical plants on the southwest coast. The penalty for all this balminess, however, is a high level of rainfall, producing the intense greenness which gives Ireland its alternative "Emerald Isle" appellation. Ireland remains unspoiled by the large-scale encroachment of industry or the brutal building programs characteristic of other nations. As a result, wildlife has flourished, and the plethora of bird and animal species makes Ireland a nature-lover's dream.

Page 8: The Dingle Peninsula, pictured from Slea Head, County Kerry.

Page 9: The black basaltic columns of the Giant's Causeway, County Antrim.

Left: A romantic view of Glendalough – "the glen of two lakes" – in County Wicklow.

Below: To the south of Dublin lie Leinster's spectacular Wicklow Mountains. In past centuries these conical granite mountains provided an inhospitable refuge for rebels beyond the Pale.

Right: The rocky indentations of the coastline around Dunquin, County Kerry, in the Dingle Peninsula.

Right: Smerwick, on the Dingle Peninsula in County Kerry, boasts both a harbor and the famous Smerwick Strand – a magnificent beach upon which it is possible to find the sparkling pieces of quartz known as "Kerry diamonds."

Opposite, top: The River Awbeg in County Cork waters its banks liberally, producing lush vegetation of an almost overwhelming greenness.

Left: Haystacks and farm buildings huddle beneath a spectacular cloud bank in Doolin, County Clare.

Above: The coastal splendor of the Iveragh Peninsula is only one of the scenic delights of the "Ring of Kerry," a circular tour of 112 miles from Killarney to Killorglin, encompassing hills, cliffs and seascapes.

Right: Cummeenduff Glen, near Killarney in County Kerry. The wooded slopes which surround its lakes and country roads make the Killarney Valley one of Ireland's loveliest beauty spots.

Left: Lough Ballynahinch, in the Connemara region of Galway – a haven for wildlife in an otherwise desolate landscape.

Below: Lough Pollacappul in County Galway is one of the county's profusion of peaceful lakes, which are much beloved of anglers for their excellent sport.

Right: The Burren – 200 square miles of County Clare – a vast area of limestone "pavements" created by glaciers and erosion. Despite its desolate appearance, however, there is enough soil to nurture an amazing variety of botanical species, from Arctic alpines to Mediterranean plants, which grow together within the pavements' narrow fissures.

Left: County Clare's formidable Cliffs of Moher – five miles of compacted dark sandstone and buhrstone grit which rise vertically 688 feet above the Atlantic Ocean. O'Brien's Tower, in the far distance, built as an observation point in 1835, is dwarfed by the cliffs' forbidding majesty. The cliffs are home to a multitude of sea birds, including gulls, puffins, kittiwakes, guillemots, and choughs.

Above: The farther west one goes in Connemara, the more wild and barren the landscape, but Galway is also rich in densely wooded hills and valleys, and in lake-strewn glens.

Above: The beach at Rosses Point, County Sligo. The point gets its name from a foreign seaman who was hastily buried at sea – so hastily, in fact, that the burial party took the precaution of providing the unfortunate man with a loaf of bread to sustain him should he still be alive.

Opposite, top: The subtle hues of the indigenous flora of Connemara bring an unexpected splash of color to the stony landscape.

Right: Extraordinarily shaped stones on the beach of Kilronan, the capital of Inishmore, which, at about eight miles long, is the largest of the Aran Islands. Besides Inishmore (Great Island) are Inisheer (East Island), and Inishmaan (Middle Island); all share the limestone rock so characteristic of the Burren.

Following pages: The market town of Clifden in County Galway, the so-called capital of Connemara, nestles in Clifden Bay against the backdrop of the Twelve Bens. *Ben* is Gaelic for "peak," while Clifden's name is derived from the Gaelic for "stepping stones" – *An Clochan.*

Left: Glencar Lough in County Sligo. Watered at one end by the Differeen River, and drained at the other by Drumcliff River, Glencar boasts a rushing waterfall which tumbles 49 feet into the depths below. Glencar was lovingly described by W. B. Yeats in his poem *The Stolen Child.*

Above, top: The Slieve League cliffs in County Donegal. These great cliffs are some of the highest in Europe, rising to nearly 2000 feet. Puffins and cormorants nest among the rocky crags, while the plant life includes Arctic alpine species.

Above: Peat by the side of the road leading to Glencolumbkille in County Donegal. Named for St. Columba of Iona (St. Columkille) who, it is said, founded a monastery here, Glencolumbkille, although poor in other natural resources, is rich in peaty soil.

Left: The amazing Giant's Causeway in County Antrim. Sixty million years ago the molten lava from spectacular volcanic activity cooled into some 38,000 basaltic, mostly hexagonal columns, to form this complex of "stepping stones." Legend has it that the causeway was built by giants to enable them to cross the water to Scotland.

Top left: The stern Mourne Mountains in County Down. The rounded granite peaks rise to a height of 2000 feet, and the lakes and streams, moorland, heathland, and profusion of wildlife, make the Mourne Mountains a walkers' paradise.

Left: An evocative view of Donegal Bay and the River Eske, which flows into Lough Eske, five miles inland.

Above: Slemish Mountain in County Antrim is a 700-foot-high extinct volcano. Pilgrims have been visiting Slemish on St. Patrick's Day – 17 March – for centuries, for it was in this area that St. Patrick spent six youthful years after his capture by Irish slave traders.

HISTORY & ARCHITECTURE

IRELAND'S HISTORY AND ARCHITECTURE go hand in hand, its monuments, religious, domestic and civic buildings all marking the traumas and triumphs of Ireland's tumultuous past.

The earliest Neolithic monuments date from between 3000 and 2000 B.C., and are found in the form of megalithic burial chambers (court cairns). Particularly numerous in the north of Ireland, the best surviving examples can be seen at Creevykeel, County Sligo, and Ballyglass, County Mayo. However, the most impressive is the passage grave at Newgrange, in the Boyne Valley, County Meath, with its extraordinary, intricate carvings. Standing stones, stone circles and mysterious dolmen bear witness to the culture of the Beaker people: the Browne's Hill dolmen outside Carlow Town, County Carlow, have a staggering 100-ton capstone, while the Burren, in County Clare, is scattered with wedge-shaped limestone tombs. The Celts left a rich religious and secular legacy. Evidence of the pagan druidic cult in the form of stone head idols can be found everywhere in Ireland, decorated with the whorls and spirals of the La Tène style. Early defensive buildings still survive in the form of ring- and hill-forts, as do some *crannogs* (artificial islands).

Nothing in the way of domestic architecture remains from the early Christian era, but many *clochans* from the seventh century still stand. Used as oratories by reclusive holy men, these stone beehive-shaped structures can be seen in the west. Another curious historical legacy are the round towers. Reminiscent of chimneys in form, they were built near churches and were used as watchtowers against the incursions of the Vikings; the round tower at Glendalough, County Wicklow is a prime example. The mingling of the Celtic and Christian artistic traditions is particularly well illustrated by Ireland's stone high crosses, in the distinctive Celtic ringed manner, carved with biblical scenes. Many crosses can be seen all over the island, but the best are probably that at Moone, County Kildare, and Muiredach's Cross at Monasterboice in County Louth. By the twelfth century Irish churches

and monasteries were being decorated in the Hiberno-Romanesque style, as seen at Cormac's Chapel on the Rock of Cashel, County Tipperary. Sadly, many fine monasteries now exist only as ruins, albeit very picturesque ones.

The Anglo-Norman invasion paved the way for the introduction of Gothic architecture, and the restored St. Patrick's Cathedral in Dublin represents this genre impressively. The secular manifestation of the invasion was the castle. In typical Norman style, the castle of Trim, County Meath is a classic example, as is Carrickfergus Castle, County Antrim, with its keep, turrets and battlements, while King John's Castle, built in 1200 in Limerick, is one of the finest specimens of fortified architecture in the country.

With the exception of Trinity College, Dublin, founded in 1592 by Elizabeth I, there was little building of note during the troubled sixteenth and seventeenth centuries, apart from that of the defensive house. English monarchs paid their soldiers with Irish land, upon which the new settlers built fortified houses, such as Ormonde Castle at Carrick-on-Suir, County Tipperary. By the eighteenth century Protestant landowners felt secure enough – and rich enough – to build magnificent houses for themselves in the fashionable Palladian style, updated into "Gothick" fantasies in the late eighteenth century. One of the finest neoclassical houses is Bantry Bay House, County Cork, built in 1740. However, Palladian architecture is best represented in Dublin, whose elegant residential squares have ensured its place as the finest large Georgian city still preserved.

Ireland kept apace with the vogue for grand municipal building in the late nineteenth and twentieth centuries, and Dublin and Belfast are especially rich in examples of this. Although perhaps not as splendid, Ireland's smaller towns possess a fine mix of interesting civic and domestic buildings, while the humble rural cottage, built of local materials – sometimes thatched, and often whitewashed – has a simple charm which is altogether Irish.

Left: The Newgrange passage grave is one of 15 Neolithic burial sites in County Meath's *Brugh na Boinne* ("palace of the Boyne") region. Believed to have been built in around 3100 B.C. (the surrounding white quartzite wall is modern), Newgrange is about 40 feet high. Inside, a 62-foot-long narrow passage leads to a great central chamber, whose corbeled roof has kept it dry for centuries, and thence to a single capstone. Precise prehistoric engineering ensured that the tunnel allows the sun to shine in each year on 21 December – the winter solstice.

Page 30: The church at Kilmalkedar in County Kerry, built in the twelfth century, is a superb example of the Hiberno-Romanesque style. It is likely that there was a pagan settlement here, for around the church can be found a number of ancient carved stones.

Page 31: This granite stone in the graveyard of Downpatrick Cathedral in County Down is said to mark the grave of St. Patrick. Although it is believed that St. Patrick founded a monastery here, there is no definite evidence that this was his final resting place. The twelfth-century Norman knight, John de Courcy, however, asserted otherwise for political reasons, claiming that he had discovered the grave, along with those of St. Columba and St. Brigid.

Left: Muiredach's Cross at Monasterboice in County Louth is considered the most perfect high cross in Ireland. Dating from the late ninth or early tenth century, the cross is covered in biblical scenes carved into the stone. Pictured here is the Crucifixion.

Below: The huge entrance stone to the Newgrange passage tomb is decorated with elegant spirals and lozenges, which are believed to have had religious symbolism in ancient times.

Right: The ruins of the monastic school at Glendalough, County Wicklow, which was founded by St. Kevin in 520 A.D. Its round tower is 100 feet high, with a doorway set 11 1/2 feet above ground level.

Opposite, top: Unfortunately, the 100-roomed eighteenth-century Powerscourt House in County Wicklow was gutted by fire in the 1970s, but the beautiful formal gardens still remain. Laid out by Daniel Robertson from 1843 to 1875, a pebble-paved terrace leads to stepped gardens in the Italianate and Japanese styles, all set against the backdrop of the imposing Sugarloaf Mountain.

Left: Merrion Square in Dublin is home to some of Europe's finest Georgian houses, which face each other across a well-maintained public park. Famous past residents include Oscar Wilde's parents, Daniel O'Connell, W. B. Yeats, and Sheridan Le Fanu.

Above: There are seven churches at Glendalough, County Wicklow, including St. Kevin's Church, with its corbeled stone roof and round steeple.

Right: Despite the overall appearance of elegant conformity, each perfectly proportioned door in Dublin's Merrion Square is somehow different from its neighbor, reflecting the personality of the owner.

Above: The three-arched O'Connell Bridge over Dublin's River Liffey. Originally called Carlisle Bridge, it was later renamed in honor of Daniel O'Connell, Ireland's "Great Liberator." In the background can be seen the domed Custom House.

Left: The majestic copper dome of the Custom House is one of Dublin's best-loved landmarks. The four decorated faces of its quadrangular base support the dome, which is surmounted by the figure of commerce. Designed by Gandon and completed in 1791, it houses the local government's customs and excise department. Sadly, it was ravaged by fire during the civil-war fighting of 1921, but has now been fully restored.

Opposite, top: Dublin's Halfpenny Bridge, which spans the River Liffey. Its name is a reminder that it was once a toll bridge. Today the crossing is free.

Right: Ireland's esteemed center of scholarship, Trinity College, Dublin, was, in fact, founded by Queen Elizabeth I of England in 1592. Its façade dates from 1759, and most of the buildings on campus were erected in the eighteenth century. The Long Room in the Old Library houses the famous twelfth-century *Book of Kells*.

Above: The imposing Lismore Castle in County Waterford has a rich history, and incorporates a medieval fortress built by King John of England in 1185. Much of its present structure dates from the nineteenth century.

Left: Blarney Castle in County Cork is one of the best examples of a medieval tower house in Ireland, and was built by Cormac Láidir in 1446. The castle is most famous, of course, for its celebrated Blarney Stone.

Right: Caher Castle in County Tipperary is believed to date from the fifteenth century, although the islet in the River Suir on which it is built was fortified from the third century.

Opposite, top: The Gallarus Oratory in County Kerry - a relic from the days of the early Christian holy men. Built in a curious boat shape, the corbeled stone keeps out the elements.

Left: Munster is not all magnificent castles, as this simple thatched cottage in County Kerry shows.

Above: The graves of victims of the mid-nineteenth-century famine at Kilronan on Inishmore in the Aran Islands.

Right: Complementing the gray desert of the Burren in County Clare are many mysterious dolmen, monuments of prehistoric times.

Left: The Water Gate and Maguire's Keep, Enniskillen's fifteenth-century castle in County Fermanagh. The Maguires were the chiefs of County Fermanagh until they were vanquished by the English in the seventeenth century.

Right: Roundstone in County Galway is a lovely nineteenth-century fishing village, which also lends its name to the nearby government-sponsored Roundstone Park – a noted craft center.

Below: Clifden, in County Galway. The well-kept shops and townhouses give some indication as to Clifden's past and present success as a market town.

Right: Boa Island is one of nearly 100 islands in Lough Erne, County Fermanagh. The old druidic traditions survived here long after Christianity had established itself in Ireland, and this ancient figure in the old cemetery testifies to a notable pagan presence. The most famous relics are the "Janus" figures, which have a face on each side.

Below: A traditional farmhouse in Connemara.

Far right: Just south of Enniskillen, County Fermanagh, is Castle Coole, the seat of the Earls of Belmore, and one of Ireland's most distinguished neoclassical houses. Built between 1790 and 1797, the castle's main block was designed by James Wyatt. Inside can be found the exquisite plasterwork ceilings of Joseph Ross.

Left: The Beaghmore Stone Circles, outside Cookstown in County Tyrone, date from the late Stone or early Bronze Age.

Top: The monumental Grianan of Aileach, in County Donegal. Commanding the hilltop of Aileach, and overlooking Lough Swilly and Lough Foyle, it is thought that this circular stone fort dates from 1700 B.C. *Grianan* means "fort" in Gaelic and, according to the *Annals of the Four Masters*, and confirmed by its 13-foot-thick walls, this was the seat of the O'Neill kings of Ulster from the fifth to the twelfth centuries. It was restored about a century ago.

Above: Parliament House, at Stormont in Belfast, is a striking example of the English Palladian style.

Above: The now-ruined Dundrum Castle in County Down was built in around 1177 as part of John de Courcy's coastal defenses. The motte-and-bailey castle encloses a circular tower - the Norman donjon.

Opposite, top: Belfast's City Hall lights up Donegall Square. This magnificent baroque-revival-style building was designed by A. B. Thomas of London, and was built between 1896 and 1906. Thomas borrowed heavily from London's St. Paul's Cathedral, as is reflected in the corner towers and 175-foot-high copper dome. It is a stirring manifestation of turn-of-the-century civic pride.

Right: Few sights are more romantic than that of the ruined Dunluce Castle in County Antrim. Built on a rugged coastal peak, in 1639 part of the supporting cliff face collapsed, taking the castle's kitchens and kitchen staff into the sea with it. Thereafter the Earls of Antrim wisely abandoned the castle to the elements.

51

Left: Castleward in County Down, situated close to Strangford Lough. Bernard Ward, the future Lord Bangor, and his wife, Anne, could not agree on which architectural style their house should follow when it was being built in the 1760s, and finally reached an amicable compromise. Bernard's preference can be seen in the neoclassical façade (pictured here), while that of his wife is displayed in the "Gothick" castellated garden front.

Above: County Down is rich in prehistoric monuments. Scattered around the countryside can be found cairns, standing stones, and strange dolmen, such as these at Legananny.

PEOPLE & TRADITIONS

IRELAND'S POPULATION IS SMALL: 3.5 million people in the Republic, and 1.5 million in Northern Ireland. Despite this, and the disruptive effect on trade and industry of centuries of strife, Ireland possesses a number of industries in which the craftsmanship is second to none. Agriculture is of prime importance to the Irish economy, and is dominated by livestock rearing; however, dairy and arable farming are also prevalent. Because of its long coastline and many waterways, all types of fishing are practiced, resulting in a notable piscatorial cuisine. Ireland is famed for its superlative brewing: Guinness stout, brewed in Dublin, is world-renowned, as is the distinctive Irish whiskey, such as that produced in the famous distillery at Bushmills, County Antrim. The textile industries are also well represented: Northern Ireland is famed for its linen, while Donegal tweed, centered on Kilcar, rivals its Scottish competitors. Northern Ireland is also home to tobacco and engineering concerns, and other mainstream industries are being developed all over Ireland.

Less labor-intensive industries are the province of the craftsmen. Traditional pursuits, including harpmaking, bookbinding, rushwork and jewelry-making, continue to thrive. Local materials are not wasted – green Connemara marble and even peat are fashioned into beautiful and collectable artifacts. Also sought after is the exquisite handworked Irish lace from centers such as Youghal in County Cork and also, of course, the highly prized glassware of Waterford, County Waterford. Aran sweaters, hand-knitted in the remote Aran Islands of County Galway, display the traditional patterns developed over the centuries, while Kinsale, County Cork, is fêted for its durable smocks.

It is impossible to generalize about the characteristics of the Irish people, but they are known for their hospitality, generosity, courtesy, and humor. As befits a race with a strong oral tradition dating back to the days of the druids, and boasting among their countrymen geniuses of poetry and prose such as W. B. Yeats and James Joyce, the Irish are garrulous, imaginative, and delight in wordplay. In the Republic, state policy has proclaimed Irish as the first official language, but despite this recent revival, the *Gaeltacht* – the area in the west where the Irish language and traditions are the strongest – had kept this heritage alive during centuries of cultural repression. The Irish are also a profoundly spiritual people. Be they Catholic or Protestant, religion is the great universal anchor, and its importance in everyday life is illustrated by the number of wayside shrines found all over the country. It is therefore hardly surprising that Knock in County Mayo, the scene of supposedly miraculous manifestations, has a religious significance equivalent to that of Lourdes. Running parallel to this is a healthy respect for mythology and super-stition. The preponderance of hair-raising stories about banshees, leprechauns and pooks, caution one to offend the fairy people, or little folk (*Daione Sidhe*), at one's peril!

Above all, the Irish know how to have a "crack" – a good time. The pace of life is unhurried, and instant relaxation can be achieved in the ubiquitous pub, to the accompaniment of lilting Irish folk music. Many towns host annual festivals, as diverse as the Rose of Tralee Festival in County Kerry, the Galway Oyster Festival, or the Wexford Opera Festival. Parades in honor of past glories are celebrated yearly, including the Ulster Unionists' Orange Day Parade, and Dublin's St. Patrick's Day Parade. Sport is followed with a passion. Popular organized sports include hurling, Gaelic football, and soccer. Greyhound racing and, more importantly, horse racing, are relished all over Ireland, boosted by the high quality of livestock bred at the National Stud at Tully, County Kildare. The nearby Curragh hosts some of Ireland's biggest races, including the Irish Sweeps Derby. More solitary pastimes enjoyed in Ireland are golf, mountain and hill walking and, for the maritime-minded, sailing, boating, surfing, windsurfing, and cruising the waterways. Sea, coarse, and game fishing are richly rewarding and much loved, as are the land-based game pursuits of hunting and shooting. "When God made time, he made plenty of it" and, as this piece of folk wisdom implies, the Irish believe that life should be enjoyed to the full.

Above: As well as being a port and car-ferry terminal, Dún Laoghaire in County Dublin is Ireland's top yachting center, the home of the Royal Saint George and Royal Irish clubs.

Left: Yachts cluster together in Kinsale harbor in County Cork, guarded by one of the two seventeenth-century "star" fortresses. The *Lusitania* was sunk ten miles to the north of here, at the Old Head of Kinsale, in 1915.

Page 54: When shopping in Dublin one is never far from one of the city's many buskers.

Page 55: Although not quite as well known as its fellow stout, Guinness, Beamish is a notable rival and worth depicting on a pub sign.

Above: Race day at The Curragh, County Kildare. The Irish are passionate about horse racing, and The Curragh, home of the Irish Sweeps Derby, is the most important racecourse in the country. Close by is the National Stud at Tully; it is said that the superb quality of the horses bred here is due to the limestone plain, which produces grass that is the world's best for building up bone.

Right: A hurling game being played between Galway and Offaly at Croke Park, County Dublin, in 1985. Hurling is Ireland's fast and exciting national game, played with hurley sticks and a leather ball. The grand finale of the hurling year is the All-Ireland Hurling Final, always held at Croke Park in September.

Left: A nun paddles discreetly at Ballinskelligs Bay in County Kerry.

Below: Neatly stacked lobster pots at Dingle, County Kerry. Dingle is the largest port in the Dingle Peninsula, and its catches are fantastically rich.

Right: According to an old Irish saying, "The only cure for drinking is to drink more." At pubs such as Murphy's Pub in Dingle, County Kerry, one can sample the whole range of Irish beverages: ale, lager, whiskey, stout, Irish coffee, or, for the very brave, poteen – illegally distilled whiskey.

Opposite, bottom: The John Long pub, one of County Kerry's many agreeable drinking establishments.

Above: The beach at Slea Head, the westernmost point of the Dingle Peninsula in County Kerry. Swimmers venturing into the Atlantic Ocean might find the sea surprisingly warm - one of the many bounties provided by the Gulf Stream.

Left: Dingle is a fertile sea-fishing ground, and its fishermen still use the small craft and traditional methods which have been employed for centuries, resisting the lure of the modern, high-tech alternatives.

Right: A wayside shrine set into a mountainside in County Kerry. Ireland is a deeply religious and predominantly Catholic country, and shrines such as this can be found in many a quiet spot.

Above: A lobster catch is unloaded at Roundstone, County Galway.

Right: The city of Galway's economic success and prime geographical position on Galway Bay make it a lively, bustling city, full of restaurants, such as that advertised by this sign, serving the freshest seafood.

Far right: Ireland's terrain is perfect for hill-walkers. Here a party of walkers pause while they negotiate the 3414 feet which make Mount Carrauntoohil, in the Macgillicuddy's Reeks in County Kerry, Ireland's highest mountain.

Above: A giant figure being assembled in honor of the Galway Oyster Festival, held every year in September. As well as the Oyster Festival, Galway hosts an arts festival, a movie festival, and plenty of race meetings.

Left: The generations live together in harmony at Moycullen in County Galway. The landscape is extremely wild, and the area's inhabitants support themselves by turf cutting and freshwater fishing; farming is a hard business.

Right: Cattle take a break on the road to Ballynahinch in County Down. In rural Ireland man and beast take life at a leisurely pace, often to the frustration of the motorist in a hurry!

Below: A sheep farmer relies on his sheepdog and donkey and cart in County Mayo. The land in this part of Ireland too poor for crop cultivation, as it mainly consists of limestone. Indeed, it was here that the nineteenth-century potato blight hit the hardest, for the potato was the only crop that would grow. Today, what agriculture there is is concentrated on fishing and sheep farming.

Above: Stacks of drying peat sods await collection. At least a sixth of Ireland's surface is covered in bog, and the peat is dug up and used as domestic fuel and garden fertilizer.

Right: A donkey train picks its way along the summit of Croagh Patrick in County Mayo. Donkeys, which are especially associated with this part of Ireland, were introduced during the Napoleonic Wars, when all the local horses were commandeered for the British Army.

Left: A signpost points the way in Gaelic in County Donegal – the county with the highest number of Gaelic speakers in Ireland.

Right: An Orange Day parade in Bangor in County Down. The Orangemen march every 12 July to the accompaniment of flute bands and Lambeg drums in commemoration of William of Orange's victory over James II at the battle of the Boyne in 1690 – here the marchers have persuaded "King William" to lead the way. The Hibernians march on 15 August. Before sectarian bitterness became too great to allow it, the two sides often lent each other instruments and equipment.

Above and left: The Old Bushmills distillery in County Antrim was founded in 1608, making it the oldest whiskey distillery in the world. Often considered to be of Scottish origin, the word "whiskey" (or "whisky") actually derives from the Irish *uisce beatha*, which means "sweet water." Although modern equipment is now used to some extent in the distilling process, Old Bushmill's three unique brands are matured in the traditional oak casks.

Left: Lough Macnean in County Fermanagh is actually two loughs, separated by a narrow strip of land upon which is sited the village of Belcoo. Fermanagh is the lakeland of Ireland, making it a fisherman's dream.

Below: Folk musicians perform at the Hearty Folk Center in Crossmaglen, County Armagh. Ireland has a rich tradition of folk music, and the talented musicians to match. Sadly, Ireland's fabled harp is rarely played nowadays.

Bottom: A weaver at work in County Donegal. Donegal is famed for its delicately colored, speckled tweed, which is handwoven from sheep's wool.

Right: Golf being played at the Royal County Down Golf Course at Newcastle, County Down. Ireland's gently rolling landscape makes it ideal for the sympathetic development of golf courses, of which there are about 200. This particular course is regarded as the best links course in the world, and is situated at the foot of the Mourne Mountains.

Left: A heavily laden donkey pulls a cart carrying his master - and the hay harvest - in County Armagh. Charming rural scenes such as this can still be seen in Ireland, in contrast to many other industrialized countries.

Above: A saddler at work at Ballymena in County Antrim. The Irish people's legendary love of horses means that a craftsman such as this will always find his skills in great demand.

Following pages: A game angler fishing on the River Strule near Omagh, County Tyrone. This area is particularly good for brown trout, sea trout and salmon. The keen angler will find abundant game, coarse, and sea fishing all over Ireland.

Left: Riders and their mounts splash contentedly along Newcastle beach in County Down. Ireland's empty beaches and hugely varied countryside, combined with the national fondness for horses, make it the ideal venue for equestrians.

ACKNOWLEDGMENTS

The publisher would like to thank Ron Callow of Design 23 for designing this book; Clare Haworth-Maden for editing it; Suzanne O'Farrell for the picture research; and Simon Shelmerdine for production. The following individuals and agencies supplied the pictures:

ULRICH ACKERMANN, pages: 7, 10(bottom), 16(top), 17, 19, 21(both), 38(top), 45(both), 54, 55, 56(top), 62(both), 65(top)

C. M. DIXON, pages: 34(top), 35, 37(top), 49(top)

© IRISH TOURIST BOARD/*BORD FAILTE*, pages: 2-3, 32-33, 34(bottom), 57(top)/Photo: Derek Cullen, page: 57(bottom)/Photos: Brian Lynch, pages: 36(top), 40, 72(bottom)/Photo: Pat Odea, pages: 22-23

© LIFE FILE/PHOTOS:
David Bayliss, pages: 64(bottom), 67(bottom)
Graham Burns, page: 66
Keith Curtis, pages: 14(top), 41(top)
Caroline Field, pages: 41(bottom), 42(top), 61
Sally-Anne Fison, pages: 59(top), 60(both)
Peter Harkin, pages: 4, 64(top)
Steve Jansen, page: 58(top)
Arthur Jumper, pages: 5, 15(top), 38(bottom), 42(bottom)
Fraser Ralston, pages: 9, 25(top), 28(top), 29, 51(bottom)
Keith Robinson, page: 15(bottom)
Cliff Threadgold, page: 16(bottom)
Flora Torrance, pages: 46(bottom), 67(top)
Robert Whistler, pages: 1, 69

PHOTOGRAPHS COURTESY OF THE NORTHERN IRISH TOURIST BOARD,
pages: 26-27, 31, 44, 46(top), 46-47, 48-49, 49(bottom), 50, 51(top), 52-53, 53, 68, 68-69, 70-71, 71(top), 72-73, 74, 75, 76-77, 78-79

©TRAVEL INK/LIFE FILE/PHOTOS:
Trevor Creighton, pages: 11, 14(bottom), 56(bottom), 62-63
Abbie Enock, pages: 10(top), 20, 24-25, 25(bottom), 28(bottom), 36(bottom), 37(bottom), 39(both), 65(bottom)
Helena Kean, page: 43(both)
David Toase, pages: 8, 12-13, 18-19, 30, 58(bottom), 59(bottom)